Essential COOKING SERIES

COMPREHENSIVE, STEP BY STEP COOKING

Meat Dishes

BUDGET
BOOKS

Food Editor: Ellen Argyriou
Project Editor: Lara Morcombe
Design: Studio Pazzo
Cover Design: Budget Books

Essential Cooking Series: Meat Dishes
This edition first published in 2008 by Budget Books
45–55 Fairchild Street
Heatherton, Victoria, 3202, Australia
www.hinklerbooks.com

10 9
13 12 11 10 09

Disclaimer: The nutritional information listed under each recipe does not
include the nutrient content of garnishes or any accompaniments not listed
in specific quantitites in the ingredient list. The nutritional information for
each recipe is an estimate only, and may vary depending on the brand of
ingredients used, and due to natural biological variations in the composition
of natural foods such as meat, fish, fruit and vegetables. The nutritional
information was calculated by using Foodworks dietary analysis software
(Version 3, Xyris Software Pty Ltd, Highgate Hill, Queensland, Australia) based
on the Australian food composition tables and food manufacturers' data.
Where not specified, ingredients are always analysed as average or medium,
not small or large.

ISBN: 978 1 7412 1939 5

Printed and bound in China

Contents

An introduction to meat dishes

Increased awareness of nutrition and health has changed our diets and the way we cook and serve meat. New trends have emerged with preference to lean cuts of meat, quick and easy recipes and the use of spices, flavourings and accompaniments drawn from international cuisines.

NUTRITIONAL VALUE

The prime nutritional benefit of meat is as a supplier of high quality protein, containing all the 8 essential amino acids required by the body and a supplier of iron. The iron in meat is readily absorbed and easily utilised by the body. With all the B group vitamins and zinc present, lean beef and veal, and trim lamb and pork are a unique combination of many essential nutrients in the one versatile, low-fat package.

Purchasing

- Only purchase the amount of meat that can be stored correctly in the space available. Check and prepare the refrigerator and freezer prior to shopping so that meat can be stored immediately on arriving home. This will include making space available, washing the meat compartment and perhaps defrosting the refrigerator.

- Overcrowding in the refrigerator and freezer will diminish its effectiveness by preventing air circulation and raising the temperature. It is always easy to find more room. Simply decant stored food into smaller containers where possible, and remove bottles and jars of preserved food such as jam, pickles, etc. to an esky.

- Keep meat cold while transporting home to prevent the growth of food spoilage bacteria. An insulated chiller-bag will suffice, or for large purchases use an esky with a cooling brick.

- To calculate the amount of meat to buy for a meal, allow 125–150 g lean boneless meat per serve.

STORAGE
Refrigerator storage

- Remove the pre-package, as plastic makes the meat sweat.

- Place on a stainless steel or plastic rack in a dish interleaved with grease-proof or waxed paper or plastic wrap, and cover to prevent the surface drying out.

- Place in the coldest part of the refrigerator at between 0° to 4°C (32°–40°F). In a refrigerator only unit the coldest part is at the bottom. In a refrigerator with an internal freezer, the coldest part is at the top just under the freezer.

Refrigerator storage guide

mince and sausages	2 days
diced meat and stir-fry strips	2–3 days
steak, chops and cutlets	2–3 days
mini roasts and boned roasting joints	2–3 days
roasting joints with bone in	3–4 days
corned beef	1 week

Vacuum packed meat

Vacuum packed meat may be stored for many weeks providing packaging is intact. Store unopened with the fat side up in a very cold refrigerator 0° to 4°C (32°–40°F) for 4–6 weeks. Once opened its shelf life is shorter than fresh meat. Use within 2 days or slice if desired, and freeze.

Freezer storage

- Trim off fat leaving a small selvedge, as fat will become rancid under long freezer storage.

- Pack chops and steaks in 1–2 layers only with freezer interleaves so that they separate easily, then place into freezer bags. Extract the air by pressing out towards the opening, fold end over and tape down. Label and date.

- Pack mince, meat cubes, stir-fry strips or sausages (left in links), in meal size quantities in freezer bags. Press out to make a wide thin package and seal.

- Freezer storage temperature should be between −15° to −18°C (5°–0°F).

- Thaw frozen meats in the refrigerator or in the microwave, never at room temperature or in water.

- Do not refreeze thawed meat.

Freezer storage guide

large roasts or joints	5–6 months
steaks and lean chops	4–6 months
cubed meat	4–6 months
neck chops	2–3 months
minced meat, sausages	1–2 months

HANDY HINTS

Grilling and pan frying

- Trim fat from the edge of steaks and chops. To prevent the meat curling up during cooking make a few small cuts around the selvedge, just past the gristle line into the meat. The gristle has no elasticity to expand as it heats; the cut prevents the meat curling.

- Season grill and pan-fried meats with pepper and herbs before cooking; sprinkle with salt during or after cooking.

- Oil sprays are a convenient and 'low fat' way of lubricating the pan and the meat before cooking.

- When grilling or barbecuing meat do not turn often. Cook the first side for 1–2 minutes to seal, turn over and cook the second side for 3–4 minutes to complete cooking.

Casseroles, stewing, braising

When browning meat cubes, heat only enough oil to coat the bottom of the pan. Meat will not brown in a lot of oil. Do not overcrowd the pan; the temperature will drop and meat juices will be extracted. Brown in batches, about 250 g (8 oz) each batch. Remove browned meat to a plate while browning remainder.

Choose a saucepan large enough to accommodate the amount of food to be cooked. The food should only half fill the saucepan to allow the rising steam and condensation cycle to assist the cooking process. Cover with a tight fitting lid.

Oven roasting

- Weigh the meat to calculate the cooking time.

- Trim thick parts of fat from the meat. Some fat cover is necessary to keep the meat moist during cooking.

- Place meat on a rack in a baking dish or place straight in the dish. Add a cup of water to the dish to protect the meat juices from charring. Retaining them in a rosy brown state gives a good gravy. When liquid dries out add a little more.

- When roast is cooked remove to a plate and cover to rest 10 minutes before carving. This gives time for the juices to settle into the meat and won't run out during carving.

- To make the gravy, skim the fat from the pan and scrape down all the brown cooked on juices from the base and sides of the pan with water or stock. Pour into a small saucepan and thicken with blended flour. A quartered onion and a few carrot chunks placed in the baking dish at the start of cooking will give extra flavour to the gravy, as will a little lemon juice added when thickening the gravy.

- Small or narrow roasts need to be cooked at 200°C (400°F, gas mark 6). Larger roasts at 180°C (350°F, gas mark 4).

- Inserting a meat thermometer with the point to reach the centre of the thickest part will eliminate guessing and ensure a roast cooked to your liking. See following table.

MARINATING MEATS

Marinades tenderise the meat, keep it moist and impart a delightful flavour.

- Marinades for meat are a combination of oil, flavourings such as fresh or dried herbs, seasonings, spices and an acid ingredient such as wine vinegar or lemon juice. The oil adds moisture to the meat, the flavouring ingredients penetrate the meat and the acid ingredients tenderise.

- Always place food in a stainless steel, glass, ceramic or hard plastic container. Aluminium must never be used.

- For a short period of time, 1 hour or less, food may be left out at room temperature. For longer marinating time or if you are making preparations in advance, place in the refrigerator.

- Turn food in the marinade so all areas come in contact with the marinade. A strong plastic container with a well fitting lid is ideal because it can be turned over at intervals to marinade all pieces.

- Never use the remaining mixture after marinating for pouring over the cooked food. Mix a fresh quantity or you may boil the remaining amount for 2–3 minutes before using.

DEGREE OF COOKING	TIME PER 500 G (1 LB)	INTERNAL TEMPERATURE AS PER MEAT THERMOMETER
Large roasts of beef, veal and lamb		
rare	15–20 minutes	60°C (140°F)
medium	20–25 minutes	70°C (158°F)
well done	25–30 minutes	75°C (167°F)
Mini roasts or beef fillet		
rare	15–20 minutes	60°C (140°F)
medium	20–25 minutes	70°C (158°F)
well done	25–30 minutes	75°C (167°F)

Pork: 30–35 minutes per 500 g (1 lb) with an external temperature of 76°C (186°F) is recommended.

Thai beef salad

INGREDIENTS

750 g (1½ lb) rump or sirloin steak
freshly ground pepper
2 handfuls mint leaves
1 large Spanish onion, thinly sliced
2 red chillies, halved, deseeded
   and very finely sliced
juice of 1 large lime or ½ lemon
2 tablespoons fish sauce
1 teaspoon sugar
lettuce leaves, whole or halved
10 cherry tomatoes
extra mint leaves to garnish
serves 4–6

PREPARATION TIME
10 minutes

COOKING TIME
10 minutes

1 Season the steak with pepper and cook under
a preheated grill for 5 minutes on each side or done to taste.
Remove, cut into very thin slices and place in a bowl.

2 In a separate bowl, combine the mint leaves with the onion,
chillies, lime or lemon juice, fish sauce and sugar. Stir well and add
to the beef slices, tossing. Arrange on a salad platter garnished
with lettuce, cherry tomatoes and extra mint leaves and serve.

NUTRITIONAL VALUE PER SERVE	FAT 3.5 G	CARBOHYDRATE 1.3 G	PROTEIN 11.1 G

Creamy sausage and bean-filled capsicums

INGREDIENTS

4 medium red capsicums (peppers)
2 teaspoons polyunsaturated oil
1 onion, finely chopped
4 thin beef sausages, poached
   and roughly chopped
2 teaspoons dried coriander
250 g (8 oz) canned tomatoes,
   chopped
2 teaspoons tomato paste
2 teaspoons ground cumin
420 g (14 oz) can red kidney
   beans, drained
1 cup (250 ml, 8 fl oz)
   thickened cream
1 cup (185 g, 6 oz) cooked rice
serves 4

PREPARATION TIME
10 minutes

COOKING TIME
50 minutes

1 Slice capsicums in half, cut out seeds and membranes. Stand in a lightly oiled baking dish.

2 Heat oil in a large, non-stick frying pan over moderate heat. Add the onions and garlic, cook for 3 minutes. Add sausages, coriander, tomatoes, tomato paste, cumin, beans and cream. Cook, stirring occasionally, for 20 minutes over moderately high heat or until mixture begins to thicken. Stir in the rice.

3 Preheat oven to 180°C (350°F, gas mark 4). Spoon mixture into prepared capsicum shells, bake in a moderate oven for 25 minutes.

NUTRITIONAL VALUE PER SERVE	FAT 9.3 G	CARBOHYDRATE 8.1 G	PROTEIN 4.2 G

Beef carbonade

INGREDIENTS

2–3 tablespoons vegetable oil
1 kg (2 lb) braising or stewing steak,
  cut into 2.5 cm cubes
1 large onion, thinly sliced
1 tablespoon plain flour
2 tablespoons soft dark
  or light brown sugar
275 ml (9 fl oz) can stout
2 cups (500 ml, 16 fl oz) beef stock
1 tablespoon tomato purée
1 bouquet garni
salt and black pepper
fresh parsley to garnish
serves 4

PREPARATION TIME
10 minutes

COOKING TIME
1¹/₂ –2 hours

1 Preheat the oven to 160°C (315°F, gas mark 2–3). Heat 2 tablespoons of the oil in a
   flameproof casserole dish. Add a third of the beef and fry over a high heat for 6–7
   minutes, turning until browned on all sides. Remove from pan and brown the remaining
   batches, adding more oil if necessary. Set aside.

2 Lower the heat, add the onion and cook for 5 minutes, stirring. Sprinkle in the flour and sugar
   and stir to a smooth paste. Pour in the stout and beef stock and bring to the boil, stirring.
   Return the beef to the dish and add the tomato purée and bouquet garni. Season and
   stir well.

3 Cover dish with lid, transfer to the oven and cook for 1¹/₂–2 hours, until the beef is tender
   and cooked through. Stir 2–3 times during cooking, adding a little water if necessary.
   Discard the bouquet garni and add salt and pepper to taste. Garnish with parsley.

NUTRITIONAL VALUE PER SERVE	FAT 4 G	CARBOHYDRATE 2.5 G	PROTEIN 11.5 G

Texan tacos

INGREDIENTS

6–8 slices lean roast beef
2 avocadoes, diced or mashed
3 tomatoes, diced
1 tablespoon chopped spring onions
(green onions)
1 clove garlic, chopped
1 tablespoon lime or lemon juice
2 tablespoons olive oil
6 drops tabasco
1 teaspoon ground coriander
1 teaspoon ground cumin
salt and freshly ground pepper
8 taco shells
2 handfuls coriander leaves, chopped
serves 8

PREPARATION TIME
5 minutes

COOKING TIME
5 minutes

1 Dice the roast beef slices and place in a bowl.

2 In a bowl, combine beef, avocadoes, tomatoes and spring onions.
In a separate bowl, combine garlic, lime or lemon juice, oil,
tabasco, ground coriander and cumin. Beat well and add to the
beef mixture. Toss lightly to combine and season to taste.

3 Crisp taco shells in a hot oven or under a preheated grill. Place
3 tablespoons beef filling in each taco shell. Top with a spoonful of
coriander leaves and serve.

NUTRITIONAL VALUE PER SERVE   FAT 14.4 G   CARBOHYDRATE 8 G   PROTEIN 3.4 G

Steak au poivre

INGREDIENTS

3 tablespoons mixed peppercorns
4 thick beef fillet steaks
(about 160 g, 5 oz each)
2 tablespoons olive oil
400 ml (13 fl oz) red wine
100 ml (3½ fl oz) water
salt
french fries or new potatoes to serve
salad to serve
serves 4

PREPARATION TIME
8 minutes

COOKING TIME
10 minutes

1 Crush the peppercorns with a pestle and mortar or the end of a rolling pin.
Brush the steaks with 1 tablespoon of the oil. Press the peppercorns around the
edge of each steak with your fingers.

2 Heat the remaining oil in a large heavy-based frying pan over a medium to
high heat. Add the steaks and cook for 5–6 minutes according to thickness,
turning once, until cooked to your liking.

3 Transfer the steaks to serving plates and keep warm. Lower the heat and pour
in the wine and water. Bring to the boil and cook for 4 minutes or until reduced
by half, stirring constantly. Add salt to taste and spoon the sauce over the
steaks to serve. Serve with french fries or new potatoes and a leafy salad.

NUTRITIONAL VALUE PER SERVE	FAT 3.4 G	CARBOHYDRATE 3.7 G	PROTEIN 7.5 G

Indonesian beef curry

INGREDIENTS

2 stalks lemon grass, peeled
  and chopped
4 tablespoons desiccated coconut,
  toasted
2 onions, chopped
2 cloves garlic, chopped
5 cm piece fresh root ginger, chopped
1 red chilli, deseeded and chopped
2 tablespoons vegetable oil
750 g (1½ lb) topside beef,
  cut into 2.5 cm cubes
1 teaspoon turmeric
400 ml (13 fl oz) can coconut milk
1 teaspoon sugar
salt
extra red chilli, deseeded
  and sliced for garnish
rice to serve
serves 4

PREPARATION TIME
8 minutes

COOKING TIME
3 hours

1 Peel the outer layers from the lemon grass stalks, then finely chop the lower white
   bulbous part. In a food processor, finely grind the toasted coconut and set aside.
   Process the lemon grass, onions, garlic, ginger and chilli to a paste.

2 Heat the oil in a frying pan and fry the paste for 5 minutes to release the flavours,
   stirring often. Add the beef, stir to coat and fry for 3–4 minutes, until sealed.

3 Add the ground coconut, turmeric, coconut milk, sugar and salt and mix well. Bring
   to the boil while stirring, then reduce the heat. Simmer, covered, for 3 hours, stirring
   from time to time, until the sauce reduces to a rich gravy. Garnish with the sliced
   chilli. Serve with rice.

| NUTRITIONAL VALUE PER SERVE | FAT 8.4 G | CARBOHYDRATE 10.5 G | PROTEIN 11.3 G |

Beef udon noodle soup

INGREDIENTS

90 g (3 oz) udon noodles
60 g (2 oz) eye fillet of beef,
  sliced very thinly
1 tablespoon thinly sliced spring
  onions (green onions)
1 tablespoon cooked tempura
  batter pieces
½ teaspoon white sesame seeds
udonji stock
1 cup (250 ml, 8 fl oz) fish stock
1 teaspoon soy sauce
1 teaspoon mirin
⅛ teaspoon sugar.
serves 1

PREPARATION TIME
10 minutes

COOKING TIME
10 minutes

1 Cook udon noodles in boiling water for 8 minutes, until tender.

2 In a saucepan, combine fish stock, soy sauce, mirin and sugar, and heat. Pour hot udonji stock into a serving bowl. Spoon in hot cooked udon noodles.

3 Overlap slices of beef onto the noodles, covering half the bowl. Add spring onions and tempura batter pieces to the soup.

4 Sprinkle sesame seeds over the soup and serve.

NUTRITIONAL VALUE PER SERVE	FAT 1.3 G	CARBOHYDRATE 15 G	PROTEIN 6 G

Steak-filled pocket breads with coriander sauce

INGREDIENTS

750 g (1½ lb) rump steak,
  sliced 3 cm thick
2 cloves garlic, crushed
90 ml (3 fl oz) red wine
3 tablespoons olive oil
1 teaspoon cracked black pepper
4 small pocket flat breads
a handful coriander leaves
  plucked off the stems
coriander butter sauce
2 cloves garlic, crushed
2 egg yolks
1 tablespoon lemon juice
2 tablespoons chopped coriander
1 tablespoon chopped parsley
125 g (4 oz) butter, melted
  and bubbling
serves 6

PREPARATION TIME
10 minutes, plus
30 minutes marinating

COOKING TIME
8–10 minutes

1 Place the steak in a flat glass dish. Mix garlic, wine, oil and pepper together and pour over the steak. Stand to marinate for 30 minutes.

2 In a food processor, place the garlic, egg yolks, lemon juice, coriander and parsley, and process for 10 seconds. With the motor running add the bubbling hot butter and process for 1 minute. Pour into a bowl and stand to cool.

3 Barbecue or grill the steak for 4 minutes each side or until cooked to your liking. Slice the steak diagonally across the grain.

4 Cut each pocket bread in half and fill the pocket with meat and coriander leaves. Whisk the sauce vigorously for 30 seconds with a wire whisk and spoon into the pocket. Serve immediately.

NUTRITIONAL VALUE PER SERVE	FAT 15.7 G	CARBOHYDRATE 8.7 G	PROTEIN 14.4 G

Pasticcio

INGREDIENTS

2 tablespoons oil
1 onion, sliced
1 kg (2 lb) beef mince
2 tablespoons tomato paste
400 g (13 oz) can tomatoes, chopped
1 cup (250 ml, 8 fl oz) water
1 tablespoon chopped
  flat-leaf parsley
1 teaspoon dried oregano
1 teaspoon sugar
1 tablespoon worcestershire sauce
1 cinnamon stick
salt and pepper
400 g (13 oz) penne pasta,
  boiled and drained
1 egg beaten
30 g (1 oz) romano cheese,
  grated for the top
béchamel sauce
90 g (3 oz) butter
75 g (2½ oz) flour
1 litre (1²/₃ pints) milk
125 g (4 oz) romano cheese,
  finely grated
4 egg yolks
salt and pepper
¼ teaspoon nutmeg

serves 10

1 Heat the oil in a frying pan. Add the onion and sauté for 5 minutes. Add the beef mince and cook for 10 minutes, breaking up the mince with a fork as it cooks.

2 Add the tomato paste, tomatoes, water, parsley, oregano, sugar, worcestershire sauce and the cinnamon stick and bring to the boil. Simmer for 45 minutes until mixture is cooked and sauce is thick. Add more water during cooking if needed. Season with salt and pepper.

3 To make the béchamel: melt the butter in a saucepan, add the flour, and stir for 1 minute. Gradually add milk while stirring. Continue to stir over heat until it thickens and boils. Remove from heat and stir in the cheese, egg yolks, salt, pepper and nutmeg.

4 Preheat the oven to 180°C (350°F, gas mark 4). In a large oiled oven-proof dish, mix together the penne and the mince mixture. Add the beaten egg to the mixture. Pour the béchamel sauce over the top and sprinkle with romano cheese. Bake in the oven for 30–45 minutes until golden set. Cut into slices and serve hot or cold, with a salad.

PREPARATION TIME
20 minutes

COOKING TIME
1½ hours

NUTRITIONAL VALUE PER SERVE   FAT **8.2** G   CARBOHYDRATE **10.9** G   PROTEIN **9.1** G

Baked lamb chops with tomato topping

INGREDIENTS

6 large lamb loin chops,
  trimmed of excess fat
fresh parsley, chopped to garnish
steamed rice to serve

marinade

3 tablespoons chopped fresh thyme
3 tablespoons olive oil
3 tablespoons red-wine vinegar
salt and black pepper

topping

500 g (1 lb) plum tomatoes
1 large green capsicum (pepper),
  deseeded and finely chopped
1 Spanish onion, finely chopped
2 large cloves garlic, finely chopped

serves 6

1 To make the marinade; place the thyme, oil, vinegar, salt and pepper in a non-metallic ovenproof dish. Add the chops and turn to coat. Cover and refrigerate for 1 hour.

2 Preheat the oven to 220°C (425°F, gas mark 7). In a bowl, place the tomatoes and cover with boiling water. Leave for 30 seconds, peel, deseed and chop.

3 In a separate bowl, mix together the tomatoes, capsicum, onion and garlic. In a baking tray, place chops and spoon over the tomato mixture. Bake for 35 minutes for medium-cooked chops, or 45 minutes for well done. Cover with foil and set aside for 5 minutes to rest. Garnish with parsley. Serve with steamed rice if desired.

PREPARATION TIME
10 minutes, plus
1 hour refrigeration

COOKING TIME
35–45 minutes, plus
5 minutes standing

NUTRITIONAL VALUE PER SERVE	FAT 4.3 G	CARBOHYDRATE 13.6 G	PROTEIN 5.7 G

Lamb and apricot casserole

INGREDIENTS

1 tablespoon sunflower oil
500 g (1 lb) lean boneless lamb leg,
  cut into 2.5 cm cubes
1 large onion, chopped
1 clove garlic, finely chopped
2 tablespoons plain flour
1 teaspoon ground coriander
1 teaspoon ground cumin
1⅓ cups (350 ml, 11½ fl oz)
  vegetable stock
150 ml (5 fl oz) red wine
225 g (7½ oz) baby button mushrooms
1 tablespoon tomato paste
1 bouquet garni
black pepper
175 g (6 oz) dried apricots
2 tablespoons chopped fresh coriander
extra coriander to garnish
broccoli to serve
rice to serve

serves 4

1 Preheat the oven to 160°C (315°F, gas mark
  2–3). Heat the oil in a flameproof casserole
  dish on stove top. Add the lamb and cook for
  about 5 minutes or until browned. Remove
  and keep warm.

2 Add the onion and garlic to the dish and cook
  for 5 minutes or until softened. Return the
  lamb to the dish with the flour, coriander and
  cumin and cook for 1 minute, stirring. Slowly
  add the stock and wine and bring to the boil,
  stirring. Stir in the mushrooms, tomato paste,
  bouquet garni and black pepper. Cover,
  transfer to the oven and cook for 1 hour.

3 Stir in the apricots and cook for a further 30
  minutes or until the lamb is tender. Remove and
  discard the bouquet garni. Stir in the chopped
  coriander. Garnish with fresh coriander and
  serve with steamed broccoli and rice.

PREPARATION TIME
15 minutes

COOKING TIME
1 hour 45 minutes

NUTRITIONAL VALUE PER SERVE   FAT 1.9 G   CARBOHYDRATE 11 G   PROTEIN 6.2 G

Honey lamb stir-fry

INGREDIENTS

500 g (1 lb) boneless lamb, cut into
  strips
3 tablespoons honey
3 tablespoons dry sherry
2 tablespoons soy sauce
1 teaspoon five-spice powder
1 teaspoon sesame oil
1 tablespoon peanut oil
2 medium carrots, cut into
  julienne strips
3 sticks celery, cut into julienne strips
200 g (7 oz) bean sprouts
45 g (1½ oz) slivered almonds
toasted sesame seeds
250 g (8 oz) cellophane noodles,
  boiled and drained
serves 4–6

PREPARATION TIME
8 minutes, plus
20 minutes marinating

COOKING TIME
12 minutes

1 In a non-metallic container, place lamb strips. Combine honey, sherry, soy sauce, five-spice powder and sesame oil and pour over the lamb. Marinate for 20 minutes. Drain off excess marinade and reserve.

2 Heat half of the peanut oil in a wok or large frying pan. Add carrot, celery, bean sprouts and almonds and stir-fry for 2–3 minutes. Remove and set aside.

3 Add remaining peanut oil and stir-fry the lamb strips in 2 batches for 2–3 minutes until well-browned. Return vegetables and almonds to the wok or pan, and toss to combine. Pour in the reserved honey marinade, toss well to coat and heat through for 2–3 minutes. Remove to a serving dish and sprinkle with sesame seeds. Serve with cooked noodles.

| NUTRITIONAL VALUE PER SERVE | FAT 8.8 G | CARBOHYDRATE 14.6 G | PROTEIN 3.6 G |

Indian meatballs
in tomato sauce

INGREDIENTS

500 g (1 lb) minced lamb
5 tablespoons natural yoghurt
5 cm piece fresh root ginger,
  finely chopped
1 green chilli, deseeded and
  finely chopped
3 tablespoons chopped
  fresh coriander
2 teaspoons ground cumin
2 teaspoons ground coriander
salt and black pepper
2 tablespoons vegetable oil
1 onion, chopped
2 cloves garlic, chopped
1/2 teaspoon turmeric
1 teaspoon garam masala
400 g (13 oz) can chopped tomatoes
150 ml (5 fl oz) water
rice to serve
serves 4

1 In a large bowl, mix together the lamb,
   1 tablespoon yoghurt, the ginger, chilli,
   2 tablespoons coriander, the cumin, ground
   coriander, salt and pepper. With wet hands,
   shape the mixture into 16 balls.

2 Heat 1 tablespoon of oil in a large saucepan.
   Add half the meatballs and cook until brown
   well all over. Remove, drain on kitchen paper
   and set aside. Repeat with remaining
   meatballs.

3 Heat the remaining oil in the pan. Add the
   onion and garlic and fry for 5 minutes or until
   softened, stirring occasionally. Stir in the
   turmeric, garam masala and remaining
   yoghurt, 1 tablespoon at a time.

4 Add the tomatoes and their juice, meatballs
   and water and bring to the boil. Partly cover
   the pan, reduce the heat and simmer for 30
   minutes, stirring occasionally. Sprinkle over the
   rest of the coriander to garnish. Serve with rice.

PREPARATION TIME
20 minutes

COOKING TIME
45 minutes

NUTRITIONAL VALUE PER SERVE	FAT 4.7 G	CARBOHYDRATE 11 G	PROTEIN 6.5 G

Lamb and sweet potato stew

INGREDIENTS

1 tablespoon olive oil
12 lamb cutlets or chump chops
750 ml (1¼ pints) lamb or
  chicken stock
2 onions, thinly sliced
750 g (1½ lb) sweet potatoes, cut into
  1 cm thick slices
300 g (10 oz) carrots, chopped
5 sticks celery, chopped
6 fresh sage leaves
4 fresh thyme sprigs
salt and black pepper
3 tablespoons pearl barley
serves 6

PREPARATION TIME
12 minutes

COOKING TIME
1 hour 45 minutes

1 Preheat the oven to 180°C (350°F, gas mark 4). Heat the oil in a large, heavy-based frying pan and fry the cutlets a few at a time for 1–2 minutes on each side to brown. Remove the cutlets, drain off the oil and add a little stock to the pan. Bring to the boil while scraping up the pan juices. Remove and add to the rest of the stock.

2 Place half the onions in a large ovenproof casserole dish. Top with one-third of the sweet potatoes, then add half the carrots and celery, and all the sage, thyme and cutlets. Season, then sprinkle over the barley. Repeat the layering and top with the remaining sweet potatoes. Pour over the stock and cover.

3 Place in the preheated oven and cook for 1½ hours or until the lamb is tender. Add more stock or water if necessary. Remove the lid for the last 15 minutes to brown the top.

NUTRITIONAL VALUE PER SERVE	FAT 7.8 G	CARBOHYDRATE 5.2 G	PROTEIN 6.3 G

Lamb with lemon and garlic

INGREDIENTS

3 tablespoons olive oil
1 kg (2 lb) lean, boneless lamb,
  cut into 2.5 cm pieces
1 Spanish onion, finely chopped
3 cloves garlic, crushed
1 tablespoon paprika
3 tablespoons finely
  chopped fresh parsley
3 tablespoons fresh lemon juice
1/2 cup (125 ml, 4 fl oz) stock or water
salt and pepper
3 tablespoons dry white wine
  (optional)
serves 3–6

PREPARATION TIME
8 minutes

COOKING TIME
60–70 minutes

1 In a large heavy-based pan, heat oil. Add half of the lamb and
brown well on all sides. Remove to a plate and repeat with
remaining lamb. Remove and cover to keep warm.

2 Stir onion into pan and cook about 5 minutes, until softened. Stir
in garlic and cook 2 minutes, then stir in paprika. Return the lamb
to the pan with any juices on plate. Add the parsley, lemon juice,
stock or water, salt and pepper. Cover tightly and cook over very
low heat for 50–60 minutes, shaking pan occasionally, until lamb
is very tender. If necessary, add wine or 3 tablespoons water.

NUTRITIONAL VALUE PER SERVE	FAT 6.4 G	CARBOHYDRATE 0.5 G	PROTEIN 14.6 G

Lamb osso bucco

INGREDIENTS

2 tablespoons plain flour
salt and black pepper
4 lamb leg shanks, trimmed
  of excess fat
2 tablespoons olive oil
1 onion, finely chopped
1 carrot, finely chopped
1 stick celery, finely chopped
400 g (13 oz) can chopped tomatoes
  with garlic and herbs
1 tablespoon sun-dried
  tomato paste
150 ml (5 fl oz) dry white wine
450 ml (14 fl oz) lamb stock
garnish
1 tablespoon chopped fresh parsley
1 tablespoon chopped fresh mint
rind (zest) of 1 lemon, finely grated
1 clove garlic, finely chopped
serves 4

PREPARATION TIME
15 minutes

COOKING TIME
2 hours

1 Preheat the oven to 160°C (315°F, gas mark 2–3). On a plate, mix together the flour, salt and pepper. Dip the lamb shanks into the mixture to coat well. Heat 1 tablespoon of the oil in a large heavy-based frying pan until hot but not smoking. Add the lamb and cook over a medium-high heat, turning frequently, until browned on all sides. Transfer to a deep ovenproof dish. Wipe out the pan with kitchen paper.

2 Heat the remaining oil in the pan. Add the onion, carrot and celery and cook over a low heat for 4–5 minutes, until softened. Add the tomatoes, tomato paste, wine and stock and bring to the boil, stirring occasionally. Pour over the lamb, cover with foil or lid and bake for 1³⁄₄–2 hours, until the meat is tender, turning it over halfway through. Season to taste.

3 In a small bowl, mix together the parsley, mint, lemon rind and garlic. Sprinkle the garnish over the lamb and serve.

NUTRITIONAL VALUE PER SERVE	FAT 4.9 G	CARBOHYDRATE 2.3 G	PROTEIN 7.3 G

Roasted leg of lamb with vegetables

INGREDIENTS

2 kg (4 lb) leg of lamb
2 cloves garlic, cut into slivers
1–2 fresh rosemary sprigs,
  cut into small pieces
salt and black pepper
500 g (1 lb) parsnips, chopped
400 g (13 oz) carrots, chopped
6 heads endive (chicory), cut into
  quarters lengthways
300 ml (10 fl oz) red or white wine
2 tablespoons red-wine vinegar
serves 6

PREPARATION TIME
10 minutes

COOKING TIME
2–2$\frac{1}{2}$ hours, plus
15 minutes resting

1 Preheat the oven to 180°C (350°F, gas mark 4). Make several incisions in the leg of lamb, using a sharp knife. Push the garlic slivers and pieces of rosemary into the incisions. Season the lamb well.

2 Arrange the vegetables in a large roasting tin and place the lamb on top. Pour in the wine and vinegar and roast for 2–2$\frac{1}{2}$ hours, until the lamb is tender, basting the lamb and turning the vegetables in the cooking juices every 30 minutes. Add a little more wine or water if necessary.

3 Transfer the lamb to a plate, reserving the cooking juices, then cover with foil and rest for 15 minutes. Carve the lamb and serve with the vegetables, with the cooking juices drizzled over.

NUTRITIONAL VALUE PER SERVE	FAT 2.5 G	CARBOHYDRATE 1.5 G	PROTEIN 9.5 G

Lamb shanks with broad beans, olives and risoni

INGREDIENTS

2 tablespoons olive oil
2 cloves garlic, crushed
4 lamb shanks
1 onion, chopped
2 cups (500 ml, 16 fl oz) beef stock
4 sprigs oregano
2 tablespoons tomato paste
2 cups (500 ml, 16 fl oz) water
100 g (3½ oz) risoni pasta
125 g (4 oz) frozen broad beans,
   thawed
160 g (5½ oz) black olives
2 teaspoons chopped fresh oregano
salt and freshly ground pepper
serves 4–6

PREPARATION TIME
10 minutes

COOKING TIME
1 hour

1 Heat oil in a large saucepan. Add garlic, lamb shanks and onion, and cook for 5 minutes until shanks are lightly browned. Add the beef stock, oregano, tomato paste and half the water. Bring to the boil, reduce heat, and cover and simmer for 45 minutes. Remove shanks, slice meat off bone, and set aside.

2 Add the risoni and remaining water, and cook for a further 5 minutes. Add broad beans, olives, meat, oregano, salt and pepper. Cook for 5 minutes, and serve.

| NUTRITIONAL VALUE PER SERVE | FAT 4.5 G | CARBOHYDRATE 5.9 G | PROTEIN 7 G |

Pork and mushroom kebabs with black olives

INGREDIENTS

1 clove garlic, finely chopped
2 tablespoons finely chopped
   flat-leaf parsley
1 tablespoon finely chopped
   pitted black olives
grated rind (zest) and juice
   from 1 fresh lime
3 tablespoons olive oil
cracked black pepper
500 g (1 lb) lean diced pork pieces
200 g (7 oz) brown mushrooms,
   cut into pieces
8 bamboo skewers, soaked
   in water for 1 hour
potato wedges to serve
salad to serve
serves 4

1 In a bowl, combine garlic, parsley, olives, grated lime rind and juice, oil and pepper. Thread pork and mushrooms onto skewers, about 3 pieces of mushroom and pork per skewer.

2 Cook on lightly oiled barbecue or grill over a medium-high heat for 5–6 minutes turning and brushing with the basting sauce until cooked to your liking.

3 Serve kebabs and spoon over the remaining basting sauce. Serve with potato wedges and salad.

PREPARATION TIME
15 minutes, plus
1 hour soaking

COOKING TIME
6 minutes

| NUTRITIONAL VALUE PER SERVE | FAT 8.7 G | CARBOHYDRATE 17.5 G | PROTEIN 9.8 G |

Warm vegetable salad with serrano ham

INGREDIENTS

2 leeks, white parts only, sliced

200 g (7 oz) shelled broad beans
or garden peas

150 g (5 oz) snow peas (mangetout)

3 tablespoons olive oil

1 clove garlic, thinly sliced

3 spring onions (green onions),
cut into 5 cm lengths

75 g (2½ oz) baby spinach

salt and black pepper

3 slices serrano ham,
cut into thin slices

2 large open-mushrooms,
very thinly sliced

few drops of lemon juice

parmesan to serve (optional)

serves 6

1 Bring a large saucepan of lightly salted water to the boil. Add the leeks, broad beans or peas and cook for 2 minutes. Add the snow peas and stir for a few seconds. Drain and set aside.

2 Add 2 tablespoons of oil to the pan and heat. Add the garlic and spring onions. Stir for a minute to soften slightly. Add the spinach and stir until it starts to wilt. Add the cooked vegetables to the pan with the remaining oil. Lightly season and fry for 2 minutes to heat through.

3 Add the ham to the pan and heat through for 1–2 minutes. Arrange the mixture on a serving plate. Scatter over the mushrooms and sprinkle with lemon juice. Shave over the parmesan, if using, and season with black pepper.

PREPARATION TIME
10 minutes

COOKING TIME
8 minutes

NUTRITIONAL VALUE PER SERVE	FAT 8 G	CARBOHYDRATE 4.1 G	PROTEIN 5.9 G

Pork and mushroom risotto

INGREDIENTS

60 g (2 oz) butter
2 tablespoons olive oil
1 onion, chopped
3 cloves garlic, crushed
250 g (8 oz) arborio rice
1 cup (250 ml, 8 fl oz) white wine
1.25 litres (2 pints) chicken stock
225 g (7½ oz) pork stir-fry,
  lightly browned
500 g (1 lb) button mushrooms, sliced
½ cup (125 ml, 4 fl oz) fresh cream
60 g (2 oz) parmesan cheese, grated
12 sprigs fresh parsley, chopped
3 tablespoons finely chopped
  green capsicum (pepper)
salt and pepper
extra parmesan to serve
serves 4

PREPARATION TIME
8 minutes

COOKING TIME
35–40 minutes

1 Heat butter and oil in a heavy-based pan. Add onions and garlic and sauté. Add rice and sauté until well-coated. Add wine and stir until absorbed

2 Add 1 litre (1⅔ pints) hot stock, ½ cup (125 ml, 4 fl oz) at a time. Stir continuously while stock is absorbed before adding the next ½ cup. This takes about 20 minutes.

3 Stir in pork, mushrooms, cream, parmesan, parsley, capsicum and remaining stock. Season with salt and pepper, cover and simmer 10 minutes.

4 Taste and adjust accordingly. Stand covered for 2–3 minutes before serving. Serve with extra parmesan.

NUTRITIONAL VALUE PER SERVE	FAT 6.7 G	CARBOHYDRATE 7.3 G	PROTEIN 5.5 G

Sweet curried pork spareribs

INGREDIENTS

1 kg (2 lb) American-style pork ribs
3 tablespoons soy sauce
1 tablespoon honey
1 tablespoon brown vinegar
2 teaspoons curry paste
3 tablespoons tomato sauce
1 tablespoon sherry
2 cloves garlic, crushed
1 tablespoon grated fresh ginger
2 tablespoons chopped parsley
2 tablespoons sweet chilli sauce
serves 3-4

PREPARATION TIME
**8 minutes, plus
3 hours or overnight
marinating**

COOKING TIME
30–40 minutes

1 Cut pork ribs into serving pieces (3–4 ribs per serve) and place into
a large, non-metallic container. In a bowl, mix together soy sauce,
honey, vinegar, curry paste, tomato sauce, sherry, garlic, ginger,
parsley and sweet chilli sauce. Pour over the ribs. Cover and
marinate for 3 hours or overnight in the refrigerator. Turn in
marinade occasionally.

2 Preheat oven to 180°C (350°F, gas mark 4). Remove ribs from
marinade and place in a baking tray. Cook for 30–40 minutes,
turning and brushing with marinade at 10 minute intervals. Serve
immediately.

NUTRITIONAL VALUE PER SERVE	FAT 13.7 G	CARBOHYDRATE 3.9 G	PROTEIN 21.7 G

Pork mince and date burgers

INGREDIENTS

500 g (1 lb) lean pork mince
45 g (1½ oz) fresh dates,
  finely chopped
1 teaspoon ground cardamom
¼ teaspoon ground cloves
½ teaspoon freshly grated ginger
grated rind and juice of 1 lime
2 tablespoons freshly chopped mint
1 egg, lightly beaten
1 medium eggplant (aubergine)
2 tablespoons olive oil
8 pieces roasted red capsicum
  (pepper)
baby rocket (arugula) leaves
onion relish (optional)
serves 4

PREPARATION TIME
**8 minutes, plus
30 minutes
refrigeration**

COOKING TIME
18 minutes

1 In a bowl, combine the pork mince, dates, cardamom, cloves, ginger, lime rind and juice, mint and egg. Mix together well. Shape mixture into 8 small patties and place onto a plate. Cover and chill for 30 minutes.

2 Cut eggplant into 1 cm thick slices. Grill on preheated grill for 3 minutes each side oruntil lightly golden, lightly brushing with 2 tablespoons of oil during cooking. Remove and keep hot.

3 Place the patties on the hot grill and cook 5–6 minutes on each side or until done.

4 Serve pork burgers on eggplant slices with capsicum, baby rocket leaves and relish.

NUTRITIONAL VALUE PER SERVE	FAT 5.3 G	CARBOHYDRATE 3.6 G	PROTEIN 8 G

Vietnamese spring rolls

INGREDIENTS

1 tablespoon oil
350 g (1–1¹⁄₂ oz) minced pork
1 tablespoon grated fresh ginger
1 tablespoon finely chopped
  spring onions (green onions)
2 tablespoons soy sauce
1 small red chilli, deseeded
  and finely chopped
2 teaspoons honey
300 g (10 oz) green prawns, peeled,
  deveined and finely chopped
90 g (3 oz) bean sprouts
1 tablespoon chopped basil
24 wonton wrappers
oil for deep frying
makes 20

PREPARATION TIME
10 minutes

COOKING TIME
10–15 minutes

1 Heat oil in a frying pan over moderate heat. Add pork, ginger, spring onions and soy sauce. Cook while stirring constantly for 3 minutes. Stir in chopped chilli, honey, prawns, bean sprouts and basil, and mix well to combine. Remove to a flat dish, spread out to cool.

2 Separate wonton wrappers. Place on work surface and place a tablespoon of filling across the corner of each wrapper. Roll up, tucking in the sides. Brush end with water to seal.

3 Heat enough oil to be 4 cm deep in a saucepan. Add the rolls a few at a time and fry until golden. Drain on absorbent paper and continue with remainder. Serve hot.

NUTRITIONAL VALUE PER SERVE	FAT 7.5 G	CARBOHYDRATE 11.4 G	PROTEIN 13.3 G

Venison with cranberry and red-wine sauce

INGREDIENTS

4 tenderloin venison steaks
  (about 185 g, 6 oz each)
2 tablespoons peanut oil
juice of ¹/₂ orange
juice of ¹/₂ lemon
¹/₂ teaspoon ground allspice
salt and black pepper
watercress to garnish
potatoes to serve
vegetables to serve

sauce

2 tablespoons peanut oil
2 shallots, finely chopped
1 stick celery, finely chopped
1 carrot, finely chopped
1 cup (250 ml, 8 fl oz) red wine
1 cup (250 ml, 8 fl oz) beef stock
a handful juniper berries
5 tablespoons cranberry sauce

serves 4

1 Put the steaks into a non-metallic dish. In a bowl, combine the oil, orange and lemon juice, allspice, salt and pepper and pour over the steaks. Cover and marinate in the fridge for 4 hours, turning twice.

2 To make the sauce; heat the oil in a saucepan. Add the shallots, celery and carrot and cook gently, stirring occasionally, for 5 minutes or until lightly browned. Add the wine, stock and berries and bring to the boil. Simmer for 20 minutes or until reduced by about half. Strain into a clean pan, add the cranberry sauce and set aside.

3 Preheat the grill to medium. Place the steaks on a rack and grill for 4–6 minutes on each side, until cooked. Reheat the sauce, stirring occasionally, until the cranberry sauce has melted. Season to taste, then spoon the sauce over the steaks and garnish with watercress. Serve on a bed of celeriac and potato mash, with some carrots or a green vegetable.

PREPARATION TIME
**8 minutes, plus
4 hours marinating**

COOKING TIME
35–40 minutes

NUTRITIONAL VALUE PER SERVE	FAT 3.8 G	CARBOHYDRATE 5.7 G	PROTEIN 8.1 G

Venison casserole with chilli beans

INGREDIENTS

2 tablespoons plain flour
salt and black pepper
750 g (1 1/2 lb) shoulder of venison,
   diced
2 tablespoons peanut oil
1 Spanish onion, finely chopped
2 cloves garlic, crushed
2 fresh green chillies, deseeded
   and finely chopped
1 tablespoon chilli powder
400 g (13 oz) can chopped tomatoes
400 ml (13 fl oz) beef stock
2 tablespoons tomato paste
2 teaspoons soft light or
   dark brown sugar
425 g (14 oz) can red kidney beans
serves 4

1 Preheat the oven to 150°C (300°F, gas mark 2). Mix together the flour, salt and pepper on a plate. Dip the venison into the mixture to coat. Heat the oil in a large flameproof casserole dish and fry the venison in batches over a medium-high heat for 5 minutes or until browned on all sides. Remove and set aside.

2 Lower the heat and add the onion with a little more oil, if necessary. Stir for 5 minutes or until lightly browned. Add the garlic, chillies and chilli powder and stir for 1 minute.

3 Add the tomatoes, beef stock, tomato paste and sugar. Bring to the boil, stirring. Add the venison, stir well and cover tightly with the lid. Transfer the dish to the oven and cook for 2 hours or until the venison is tender, stirring twice and adding the kidney beans for the last 30 minutes of cooking.

PREPARATION TIME
10 minutes

COOKING TIME
2 1/4 hours

| NUTRITIONAL VALUE PER SERVE | FAT 2.5 G | CARBOHYDRATE 4.7 G | PROTEIN 9.2 G |

Rabbit and onion casserole

INGREDIENTS

750 g (1½ lb) rabbit portions
375 ml (12 fl oz) dry white wine
3 sprigs fresh oregano
3 bay leaves
1/3 cup (80 ml, 2½ fl oz) olive oil
225 g (7½ oz) baby onions,
    peeled and halved
6 cloves garlic, unpeeled
1 tablespoon paprika
170 ml (5½ fl oz) chicken stock
125 g (4 oz) black olives
salt and freshly ground black pepper
fresh oregano sprigs, to garnish
crusty bread
serves 4

PREPARATION TIME
**10 minutes, plus
overnight marinating**

COOKING TIME
1½ hours

1 In a large bowl, combine rabbit, wine, oregano and bay leaves. Cover, and refrigerate overnight. Drain the rabbit and reserve the marinade. Preheat oven to 180°C (350°F, gas mark 4).

2 Heat the oil in a large frying pan and brown the rabbit a few pieces at a time on both sides. Remove the rabbit and place in a casserole dish.

3 Brown the onions and garlic in the pan. Once golden, add the paprika. Stir continuously for 2 minutes. Add the stock and reserved marinade. Bring to the boil. Pour onion and stock mixture over rabbit. Add olives, and season with salt and pepper.

4 Cover and bake in oven for 1¼ hours or until rabbit is cooked and tender. Garnish with oregano sprigs and serve with crusty bread.

NUTRITIONAL VALUE PER SERVE	FAT 5.4 G	CARBOHYDRATE 7.6 G	PROTEIN 10.2 G

Glossary

Al dente: Italian term to describe pasta and rice that are cooked until tender but still firm to the bite.

Bake blind: to bake pastry cases without their fillings. Line the raw pastry case with greaseproof paper and fill with raw rice or dried beans to prevent collapsed sides and puffed base. Remove paper and fill 5 minutes before completion of cooking time.

Baste: to spoon hot cooking liquid over food at intervals during cooking to moisten and flavour it.

Beat: to make a mixture smooth with rapid and regular motions using a spatula, wire whisk or electric mixer; to make a mixture light and smooth by enclosing air.

Beurre manié: equal quantities of butter and flour mixed together to a smooth paste and stirred bit by bit into a soup, stew or sauce while on the heat to thicken. Stop adding when desired thickness results.

Bind: to add egg or a thick sauce to hold ingredients together when cooked.

Blanch: to plunge some foods into boiling water for less than a minute and immediately plunge into iced water. This is to brighten the colour of some vegetables; to remove skin from tomatoes and nuts.

Blend: to mix 2 or more ingredients thoroughly together; do not confuse with blending in an electric blender.

Boil: to cook in a liquid brought to boiling point and kept there.

Boiling point: when bubbles rise continually and break over the entire surface of the liquid, reaching a temperature of 100°C (212°F). In some cases food is held at this high temperature for a few seconds then heat is turned to low for slower cooking. See simmer.

Bouquet garni: a bundle of several herbs tied together with string for easy removal, placed into pots of stock, soups and stews for flavour. A few sprigs of fresh thyme, parsley and bay leaf are used. Can be purchased in sachet form for convenience.

Caramelise: to heat sugar in a heavy-based pan until it liquefies and develops a caramel colour. Vegetables such as blanched carrots and sautéed onions may be sprinkled with sugar and caramelised.

Chill: to place in the refrigerator or stir over ice until cold.

Clarify: to make a liquid clear by removing sediments and impurities. To melt fat and remove any sediment.

Coat: to dust or roll food items in flour to cover the surface before the food is cooked. Also, to coat in flour, egg and breadcrumbs.

Cool: to stand at room temperature until some or all heat is removed, e.g. cool a little, cool completely.

Cream: to make creamy and fluffy by working the mixture with the back of a wooden spoon, usually refers to creaming butter and sugar or margarine. May also be creamed with an electric mixer.

Croutons: small cubes of bread, toasted or fried, used as an addition to salads or as a garnish to soups and stews.

Crudite: raw vegetable sticks served with a dipping sauce.

Crumb: to coat foods in flour, egg and breadcrumbs to form a protective coating for foods which are fried. Also adds flavour, texture and enhances appearance.

Cube: to cut into small pieces with six even sides, e.g. cubes of meat.

Cut in: to combine fat and flour using 2 knives scissor fashion or with a pastry blender, to make pastry.

Deglaze: to dissolve dried out cooking juices left on the base and sides of a roasting dish or frying pan. Add a little water, wine or stock, scrape and stir over heat until dissolved. Resulting liquid is used to make a flavoursome gravy or added to a sauce or casserole.

Degrease: to skim fat from the surface of cooking liquids, e.g. stocks, soups, casseroles.

Dice: to cut into small cubes.

Dredge: to heavily coat with icing sugar, sugar, flour or cornflour.

Dressing: a mixture added to completed dishes to add moisture and flavour, e.g. salads, cooked vegetables.

Drizzle: to pour in a fine thread-like stream moving over a surface.

Egg wash: beaten egg with milk or water used to brush over pastry, bread dough or biscuits to give a sheen and golden brown colour.

Essence: a strong flavouring liquid, usually made by distillation. Only a few drops are needed to flavour.

Fillet: a piece of prime meat, fish or poultry which is boneless or has all bones removed.

Flake: to separate cooked fish into flakes, removing any bones and skin, using 2 forks.

Flame: to ignite warmed alcohol over food or to pour into a pan with food, ignite then serve.

Flute: to make decorative indentations around the pastry rim before baking.

Fold in: combining of a light, whisked or creamed mixture with other ingredients. Add a portion of the other ingredients at a time and mix using a gentle circular motion, over and under the mixture so that air will not be lost. Use a silver spoon or spatula.

Glaze: to brush or coat food with a liquid that will give the finished product a glossy appearance, and on baked products, a golden brown colour.

Grease: to rub the surface of a metal or heatproof dish with oil or fat, to prevent the food from sticking.

Herbed butter: softened butter mixed with finely chopped fresh herbs and re-chilled. Used to serve on grilled meats and fish.

Hors D'Oeuvre: small savoury foods served as an appetiser, popularly known today as 'finger food'.

Infuse: to steep foods in a liquid until the liquid absorbs their flavour.

Joint: to cut poultry and game into serving pieces by dividing at the joint.

Julienne: to cut some food, e.g. vegetables and processed meats into fine strips the length of matchsticks. Used for inclusion in salads or as a garnish to cooked dishes.

Knead: to work a yeast dough in a pressing, stretching and folding motion with the heel of the hand until smooth and elastic to develop the gluten strands. Non-yeast doughs should be lightly and quickly handled as gluten development is not desired.

Line: to cover the inside of a baking tin with paper for the easy removal of the cooked product from the baking tin.

Macerate: to stand fruit in a syrup, liqueur or spirit to give added flavour.

Marinade: a flavoured liquid, into which food is placed for some time to give it flavour and to tenderise. Marinades include an acid ingredient such as vinegar or wine, oil and seasonings.

Mask: to evenly cover cooked food portions with a sauce, mayonnaise or savoury jelly.

Pan-fry: to fry foods in a small amount of fat or oil, sufficient to coat the base of the pan.

Parboil: to boil until partially cooked. The food is then finished by some other method.

Pare: to peel the skin from vegetables and fruit. Peel is the popular term but pare is the name given to the knife used; paring knife.

Pith: the white lining between the rind and flesh of oranges, grapefruit and lemons.

Pit: to remove stones or seeds from olives, cherries, dates.

Pitted: the olives, cherries, dates etc. with the stone removed, e.g. purchase pitted dates.

Poach: to simmer gently in enough hot liquid to almost cover the food so shape will be retained.

Pound: to flatten meats with a meat mallet; to reduce to a paste or small particles with a mortar and pestle.

Simmer: to cook in liquid just below boiling point at about 96°C (205°F) with small bubbles rising gently to the surface.

Skim: to remove fat or froth from the surface of simmering food.

Stock: the liquid produced when meat, poultry, fish or vegetables have been simmered in water to extract the flavour. Used as a base for soups, sauces, casseroles etc. Convenience stock products are available.

Sweat: to cook sliced onions or vegetables, in a small amount of butter in a covered pan over low heat, to soften them and release flavour without colouring.

Conversions

Measurements differ from country to country, so it's important to understand what the differences are. This Measurements Guide gives you simple 'at-a-glance' information for using the recipes in this book, wherever you may be.

Cooking is not an exact science – minor variations in measurements won't make a difference to your cooking.

EQUIPMENT

There is a difference in the size of measuring cups used internationally, but the difference is minimal (only 2–3 teaspoons). We use the Australian standard metric measurements in our recipes:

1 teaspoon ....5 ml   1 tablespoon....20 ml
1/2 cup......125 ml   1 cup.....250 ml
4 cups...1 litre

Measuring cups come in sets of one cup (250 ml), 1/2 cup (125 ml), 1/3 cup (80 ml) and 1/4 cup (60 ml). Use these for measuring liquids and certain dry ingredients.

Measuring spoons come in a set of four and should be used for measuring dry and liquid ingredients.

When using cup or spoon measures always make them level (unless the recipe indicates otherwise).

DRY VERSUS WET INGREDIENTS

While this system of measures is consistent for liquids, it's more difficult to quantify dry ingredients. For instance, one level cup equals: 200 g of brown sugar; 210 g of castor sugar; and 110 g of icing sugar.

When measuring dry ingredients such as flour, don't push the flour down or shake it into the cup. It is best just to spoon the flour in until it reaches the desired amount. When measuring liquids use a clear vessel indicating metric levels.

Always use medium eggs (55–60 g) when eggs are required in a recipe.

OVEN

Your oven should always be at the right temperature before placing the food in it to be cooked. Note that if your oven doesn't have a fan you may need to cook food for a little longer.

MICROWAVE

It is difficult to give an exact cooking time for microwave cooking. It is best to watch what you are cooking closely to monitor its progress.

STANDING TIME

Many foods continue to cook when you take them out of the oven or microwave. If a recipe states that the food needs to 'stand' after cooking, be sure not to overcook the dish.

CAN SIZES

The can sizes available in your supermarket or grocery store may not be the same as specified in the recipe. Don't worry if there is a small variation in size – it's unlikely to make a difference to the end result.

dry		liquids	
metric (grams)	imperial (ounces)	metric (millilitres)	imperial (fluid ounces)
		30 ml	1 fl oz
30 g	1 oz	60 ml	2 fl oz
60 g	2 oz	90 ml	3 fl oz
90 g	3 oz	100 ml	3 1/2 fl oz
100 g	3 1/2 oz	125 ml	4 fl oz
125 g	4 oz	150 ml	5 fl oz
150 g	5 oz	190 ml	6 fl oz
185 g	6 oz	250 ml	8 fl oz
200 g	7 oz	300 ml	10 fl oz
250 g	8 oz	500 ml	16 fl oz
280 g	9 oz	600 ml	20 fl oz (1 pint)*
315 g	10 oz	1000 ml (1 litre)	32 fl oz
330 g	11 oz		
370 g	12 oz		
400 g	13 oz		
440 g	14 oz		
470 g	15 oz		
500 g	16 oz (1 lb)		
750 g	24 oz (1 1/2 lb)		
1000 g (1 kg)	32 oz (2 lb)	*Note: an American pint is 16 fl oz.	

cooking temperatures	°C (celsius)	°F (fahrenheit)	gas mark
very slow	120	250	1/2
slow	150	300	2
moderately slow	160	315	2–3
moderate	180	350	4
moderate hot	190	375	5
	200	400	6
hot	220	425	7
very hot	230	450	8
	240	475	9
	250	500	10

Index

Essential COOKING SERIES

COMPREHENSIVE, STEP BY STEP COOKING

Essential COOKING SERIES
COMPREHENSIVE, STEP BY STEP COOKING
Baking

Essential COOKING SERIES
COMPREHENSIVE, STEP BY STEP COOKING
Chicken Meals

Essential COOKING SERIES
COMPREHENSIVE, STEP BY STEP COOKING
Salads & Greens

Essential COOKING SERIES
COMPREHENSIVE, STEP BY STEP COOKING
Soups & Hors D'Oeuvres

Essential COOKING SERIES
COMPREHENSIVE, STEP BY STEP COOKING
Meat Dishes

Essential COOKING SERIES
COMPREHENSIVE, STEP BY STEP COOKING
Finger Food

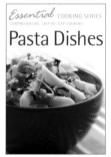

Essential COOKING SERIES
COMPREHENSIVE, STEP BY STEP COOKING
Pasta Dishes

Essential COOKING SERIES
COMPREHENSIVE, STEP BY STEP COOKING
Grilling & Barbecuing

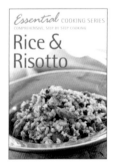

Essential COOKING SERIES
COMPREHENSIVE, STEP BY STEP COOKING
Rice & Risotto

Essential COOKING SERIES
COMPREHENSIVE, STEP BY STEP COOKING
Vegetarian Dishes

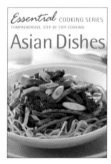

Essential COOKING SERIES
COMPREHENSIVE, STEP BY STEP COOKING
Asian Dishes

Essential COOKING SERIES
COMPREHENSIVE, STEP BY STEP COOKING
Stir-Fry